Mind Shaper

Mind Shaper

Faith's Pivotal Role in Altered Cultures

By
Jennifer P. Lumley

iUniverse, Inc.
New York   Bloomington

Mind Shaper
Faith's Pivotal Role in Altered Cultures

Cover, Graphics and Photographs by Maurice G. Fletcher and Jennifer Lumley. Illustrations by Maurice G Fletcher.

iUniverse books may be ordered through booksellers or by contacting:

iUniverse
1663 Liberty Drive
Bloomington, IN 47403
www.iuniverse.com
1-800-Authors (1-800-288-4677)

ISBN: 978-1-4401-3090-8 (sc)
ISBN: 978-1-4401-3091-5 (ebook)

Printed in the United States of America

iUniverse rev. date: 03/19/2009

EPIGRAPH

"I can do all things through Christ who strengthens me"

Philippians 4:13

"Emancipate yourself from mental slavery"

Honourable Robert Nesta Marley

'A conscious determination to orderly arrange the contours of life choices necessary to be more enlightened and to perform above expectations.'

PREFACE

All beings have unquestionably different talents and abilities and it is this distinction that affords people the opportunity to choose one vocation over another. It is, however, within everyone's power to do absolutely nothing.

A most favourable set of circumstances came about and it would have been impolitic on my part to have ignored all the signals indicating that now, more than ever, is the time to express my inner self. My writings are an intrinsic part of my existence and sharing my poems is a small part of a big vision, a story of Montego Bay and some world history.

Never mind the fact that Jamaica is smaller than all of the state of Connecticut. We are movers and shakers in our music, food, mode of dress, customs, spiritedness and attitude. America was surprised when I arrived with my island mystique, amused at my so-called English accent and taken aback with all that I had learned in Jamaica. I strive to continuously inspire and stimulate those around me through poetry, meditation, music, dance and laughter.

Make no mistake, Jamaicans are a proud people and usually very well rounded. It was not uncommon to see me leaving the tennis court, racquet in hand, clutching my Bible, heading for Youth Group Meeting at the church and my Bob Marley record that I purchased with my lunch money, carefully secured between my school books. I am physical, spiritual, musical and more. Our youth today, are just as multifarious; their beauty can shine with careful encouragement, gentle persuasion and positive, elevated reinforcement.

Jamaica became an independent nation from colonialism shortly after I was born. I was taught by British and British-trained, Jamaican teachers whose roles encompassed life skills, not on the curriculum. Discipline could be meted out by any adult in or out of school. I hope MIND SHAPER will remind family members of who is parent and cause an awakening through that knowledge. That is an education unto itself. Reading does matter, respect goes a long way and responsibility for action is ineluctable. The art of conversation has almost been forgotten; many never knew healthy discussions. MIND SHAPER is designed to have a cognitive impact on its readers and bring back table talk, amongst other things.

My keen sense of purpose has served to galvanize the reasons for this compilation. A rich and beautiful heritage is what I hope has been captured and shared in my effort. It is a bit disheartening, however, to witness the sordid behavior that has entrenched the hearts of young people and jaundiced their acceptance of fragmented materialistic ideals. These are tomorrow's leaders; this is a global epidemic. We have to dedicate more time to ameliorate the status quo while we go through life's labyrinth. One of my intentions is to help people make sensible choices, have solid plans, set achievable goals and find the means by which to accomplish their vision.

No longer can I be comfortably ensconced in believing that my writing is for me – private. We all have to make a conscious determination to orderly arrange the contours of life choices necessary to be more enlightened and to perform above expectations, thus my publication for distribution and education…MIND SHAPER!

About The Author

Born in Montego Bay, Jamaica, a middle child of six, always asking "Why?" and having a passion for poetry since elementary school days. Montego Bay High School for girls has made her more aware of many other famous writers including Wordsworth, Coleridge and Chaucer to name a few. Then of course on radio and television, Jamaica's First Lady of Comedy, Miss Lou, who so beautifully spoke and wrote the native tongue, patois, led Jennifer to write many unrecorded plays and poems of her own. Despite harsh criticism from her mother, that she would never pass her GCE English exams because of how 'badly' she wrote and recited those patois poems, Jennifer's love for this new art form continued. She passed her English exams in flying colors and has continued with her love for the English Language as was taught by the British. To date, her mother will be the first to hear and share the uncommon words piled high in Jennifer's vocabulary, whenever she hears someone else using them. Additionally, Jennifer has, on several occasions, served as a Motivational Speaker, Legislative Representative, Mentor, Guest Lecturer, High School Graduation Guest Speaker, International College Representative, High School Delegate, President of her High School Alumnae Association (New York) and in that capacity, has been interviewed on several radio stations both in New York and Jamaica. This poet has also Interviewed Jamaica's Prime Minister, Hon. Bruce Golding and the Minister of Tourism, Hon. Ed Bartlett, on behalf of local reggae news stations. (presently run on Youtube)

For most of her professional years, the author traded securities and sold traditional retail bank products. As a licensed Financial Specialist, she belonged to several professional and Non-Profit organizations, including, but not limited to, the National Association of Female Executives, International Consortium of Caribbean Professionals, National Association of Poets and the All Islands Association.

The Author can always be relied upon for a smile when she helps you to take a real look at life through her eyes. "Things could be better...or worse." She profoundly believes, however, that we are here to help each other through this madness, thus her role in life as MIND SHAPER, creating and encouraging good thoughts that emanate not just from the mind, but also from the soul.

Dedication

To the Supreme Being; praises and adoration.

He gave me to Mamie, Amy, Mother, Friend, from whom I have learned family values, industry, laughter and love of dance.

My Aunt Gloria, confidante, prim and proper, still bats her eyes and purses her lips. She's glorious!

Acknowledgements

1) Maurice Fletcher whose invaluable critique and tireless effort to perfect each illustration, made my work more worth the while; and whose wisdom kept me abreast of the updated and additional meanings of Jamaican words. Maurice also provided a great deal of moral support.

2) Hon. Louise Bennett Coverley, (Miss Lou - deceased) Jamaica's First Lady of Comedy, who provided the inspiration and the foundation upon which to dream and act on the dream. Her beauty lives on.

3) To the many friends and associates, who, over the years, have trusted me on their stages, in front of their podiums or in their pulpits, to deliver my oral presentations for a variety of events. To those who were brave enough to call me again to do same, I am grateful.

I am particularly thankful to those who had faith in me, trusting that I could make a speech sound better, or believing it would have more impact if I helped them to construct their thought on paper. Thank you all for your confidence. You actually nurtured me to get better at the art, over time with practice.

4) My friends and family who have listened over and over again to my thoughts on paper, sometimes late in the day, when I just needed an ounce of encouragement to continue my quest and I know they needed their rest, I am indebted to you. Thank you, again.

5) Strange but true, Mrs. Crick at Montego Bay High School almost made me dislike English classes. Today I am thankful for her efforts and I think she would be pleased to know that I, Jennifer P. Lumley, honed in on the skills that she knew I possessed. I did not waste her time... or mine.

6) My cat Diamond

Table of Contents

Section 3) SPIRITUAL

Section 4) LIFE

Section 5) NATURE

Section 6) PRAYERS & MEDITATION

Section 7) BRAWTA

Section 1) BEAUTY

Warm

Warm, kind curtain
Cool and calm
Flowing free
Free from harm
Shelter in the misty morn
Crown me while I move around
Let me hear all musical sounds
Captivate my soul at last
How I managed in the past
It's hard to tell, hard to know
Never ever had it flow
Brown and black and grey and white
Freckles showing bright at night
Great body moves, ooh nice and slow
Fast and elegant but now it grows
On a level playing field
A head full of locks
Locks that act just like a shield
And thoughts, fresh ideas
Flowing forth again, brown sugar
Easy-going, educated, sharing
Crazy, crazy, crazy…caring.

Jennifer P. Lumley

A Wedding Tribute

Arms like wings that flashed to and fro
Caressing her breasts and then letting go
Freeing the love that she holds so dear
Knowing she loves and loves without fear

Pointy toed and flashy smile
Her white skirt spreads across the mile
The room is silenced with her every move
Drenched with this tribute; she knows her groove

A sharp glance shoots across the room
Everyone thinks it's their personal tune
Dancer's tribute is to the bride and groom
She reigns supreme in her radiant bloom

Applause from the guests shows real satisfaction
Never seen such a show, never seen that reaction
She's done and she saunters over to her seat
A state of satisfaction; a feeling complete.

Sexy Granny

You could become a grandmother
And wear ugly granny clothes
Or you could simply dress right up
And lead men by the nose
And make them follow all commands
Smile when you tell them so
And get complements for doing nothing
And travel to and fro

You could take all the grandchildren
On picnics and on trips
Or pay for their expensive toys
These are this grandmother's tips
Go to the gym and there obtain
Your own handsome, personal trainer
He knows your aim and helps your game
This is nothing; it's a no-brainer

But you could sit and read or write
Books by the score for others
Or put bright orange lipstick on
And get men hot and bothered
Grandma you could make hot oatmeal
Bake chocolate chip cookies too
Wait for grandkids to come for soup
Or go out and get a new hairdo

Enjoy your pretty flower garden
Take a trip down to the beach
Wear sexy jeans and sandals
For womanhood you've reached
Grandmothering is so much fun
Eat out, go dancing, make a call
Don't let being a grandmother
Stop you from having a ball.

Beauty by the Sea

Shouldn't have said what I just said
Wet hands, cold feet, sweaty forehead
Don't watch me at this grueling time
Hear not my words, it's not a rhyme

Us in the sun, toes in the sand
Lips on my lips, walk holding hands
Say what, the tour bus leaves at five?
Guess we'll them see when they arrive

My shy smile and my racing heart
Is this thing real or just a thought?
Aruba has always appealed to me
But look at this beauty by the sea

Dark flowing hair and sex appeal
Sensual, smart, good looks…a deal
My height and hers match to a tee
Blue ocean waters come to me

Imagination's fabulous sometimes
Though I haven't a nickel or a dime
Nor passport or the fortitude
To say this to my gal Gertrude.

Jennifer P. Lumley

No First Name

Red breasts, nipples
Hair that ripples
Each lock unique
A whole boutique
Pick up and choose
No one is loose
It is a lock;
Gold, bronze, grey, black
No one's the same
Each has a name
You don't dare call
Look how they fall
Down his strong chest
Neck, shoulders and breasts
Smile, touch, feel, dart
Tennis, music, taxes, chart…M.A.N.

Faith

Hour glass body, chiseled calves
Decorating, Planning, Writing
Supportive, Eager, Understanding, Funny
Jenekins.

Section 2) LOVE

A Tribute to Fathers

From Vietnam to Nicaragua these people are real fighters

They're also Chemists and Presidents and some are famous Writers

They have a wide variety of jobs from Actors to Engineers

They're the Computer operators, Fishermen and Baseball players

Of course, there are the ones we call our best and favorite Teachers

Then there are Plumbers and Bus drivers and yes, there are the Preachers.

The Old man, Pop, Daddy and Pa are only a few of his names

He has troubles too you know but will always find time for games.

He'll come home from a long, hard day looking very tense and serious

But when you poke fun at the hole in his socks, the situation becomes hilarious

Today we honor and praise these men; they're all to be remembered

Not only on Fathers' day, but from January to December

So here's to those fine men- all of you; you're all appreciated

Not just a kiss and a tie and "Hey Dad, goodbye" this year it's "I'm glad we're related".

Your Kindness

Your kindness and your caring ways
Brought happiness these past six days

You must do the things you must
My heart believes, knows and trusts

That somewhere in your time away
Your thoughts will somehow come my way

Already you're missed, but with legs kissed
Walk on, don't go astray!

Know Me!

Faith loves with affection.
Faith loves affection.

I Do

Pensive, but not so hard to understand
Scruffy, grey-beard engineer
Transformed into "gentle" man
The deep set eyes and one wrinkled brow
Have you in wonderment at just how
He knows all that he knows and does all he does
And yet an easy-going character
Sparks the most radiant smile
Contagious, in a sense, because
The deep set eyes remain sexy
The one wrinkled brow is gone
And light heartedness fills the air.
You want to love him…
I just do.

Maurice

Deep-set eyes, wrinkled brow
Teaching, encouraging, studying
Pensive, brilliant, calm, accepting
Scrappy.

Angel Hair

Except for wings, there came another angel
This one in full view and a look of great concern
The one before, I heard and my vision was blurred
But they did not allow the time to pass and run away from them
Another call was placed on them to take action.

The smell of rubbing alcohol evaporated from my brow
And soothingly once again she re-applied it
Till tears almost came from my eyes, not from crying
Only from the strong but gentle disappearance of the liquid
That caressed me back to strength.

Until the first angel appeared again
So now I have the two; an audience all to myself
And charm emanating from their countenances
Although understanding the complexity of their successful labor

The first, a short, girlish, cherub-type female
With the neatest of braids pressed tight against her scalp
Even-toned, black, velvet skin and pearly white teeth
The second, a Jamaican-Indian type; smaller in stature
And gentle-natured, fanning me to make sure I got enough air

Eyes, bright; and one tooth slightly discolored
In the hint of a smile she gave
Her hair gently cascading down her back from a ponytail
Good sent these angels. I wonder if they know.

Jungle Sounds

Jungle sounds, whispers true
Is it so? It is so, I know!
I wish you would have told me so
Finding out made me raise my brow
At the new understanding of what I know.
I know what the old understanding was
I know what my obligations are elsewhere
I know that one day it might just happen
I know that you have always been honest
I know that I would still remember you
I know, I know, I know, I know, I know!!!

The sight was one thing, the feeling I know
I have felt it before. It came unexpectedly harsher
For you were always understanding and
Carefully graceful in manner and moods.
I know you cry, I've seen it for myself
I know you cry because you told me so
I know you hurt when I depart to home.
Your gentle caress, tiny as it were, protected me
Lion of the jungle.
Even if it were a kiss on the forehead
Or a warm embrace, I feared no one.

I knew no evil would befall me, simply because
I knew that I had you – sometimes.
Bruised, now I reflect upon the situation for
I know you are even more bruised, since
Soon you may have to make a decision.
Who says it will work? I will be loving you always.
I know, even if you told me no
I know I will
Accept me for who I am. You will.
I know!

Jennifer P. Lumley

Three Steps

Man is loving her oh so much
Lady turned woman; she's got the touch
What can I say feel or think?
Words, touch and thoughts take me to the brink

The bod is so tempting
It's hard; hard to resist
Clothes should be rending
But no, let's just kiss

Man is loving her, oh so smooth
Lady turned dancer, she's got the groove
Waltz her and rock her, spin her on the floor
Three step, don't move her…now swing her some more

Looks great in clothes, where is my mind?
Think I'll embrace her, looks fair, looks fine.

At Last

MFletch pro
The one I know
Some time ago
Just left and so
The other day
I saw a way
A style so neat
Oh! Quite unique
My head went hot
Look who I've hot
In my life again
A king to reign
Classy, not vain
Nothing to lose
All to gain
Willing to try
I'm on a high
Did not smoke
This is no joke
He wants to come
I want to roam
Together at last
Much time has passed
Together again
Forever, for good, at last.

Jennifer P. Lumley

Seek, Don't Hide

The damsel's looking around
The song she likes is playing now

Emerge from whence you hide your face
Reveal to me your dancing pace

Heaven is not hidden far from you
Earth is flaming with passion true

Pour out your soul with grace and passion
She will receive it in fine form and fashion.

The harshness of the winters in New York sometimes seems particularly unbearable when one is alone.

In The Cold

In the cold and lonely darkness of the room
Sits a broken soul wondering about the gloom
That hovers like heavy grey clouds, uncertain
Not grey like sweat pants or dust that sits on the curtain

Freshly laundered clothes, folded and mismatched
Lingering feelings on the three year affair, now detached
Empty heart, empty cupboard, big old empty house
Married now distant friendship only; no spouse

No spouse, no husband, no friend close by
No caring, no sharing, no giving, that's why
No man of my own, to take care of those needs
Those needs must be addressed, with utmost speed

Care for your wife, your lover, your friend
Don't let "not caring" bring this to an end
An end is so final, but that's how it will be
If you don't care for your baby, your Honey, me

Go discover the ways to keep this together
If it matters to you, then you must weather
The storm winds that blow her farther away
Put your full deck on the table if you want her to stay

The hiss of the steam from the old radiator
The sultry Jazz songs like Ray Charles at the theater
Dim lights from a distance, the cold in the air
Sets the tone for a heartbreak from a real love affair

Sometimes we get too busy, too occupied to know
Relationships need a foundation and nurturing to grow
Attention and a thorough understanding
Of each others' position, so there will be no "miss-handling"

Deep, dark, dull life
No fun; fuss and strife
Too heavy to bear anymore
Sorry, so sorry ***mi amore.***

God loves us

Now I know loving for love is in me
Merely reflecting what God wants to be
He stripped us of some things and started anew
A program, a process, from His point of view

He kept us and cleansed us, like valuable stones
Headaches and heartaches and pains in our bones
But just when we thought, no Jen, no Fletcher
God sent you to New York to come and fetch her

There is nothing except excitement in my heart
The distance between us is our head start
To love one another, to keep safe from harm
If it's hot there or cold here, our hearts will be warm

And when at last our hearts unite
We'll see that time has made everything right
For us to be together from now on
To share love forever, e'en when time itself is gone.

Section 3) SPIRITUAL

Peace for Evermore

P is for the Prince of Peace
That God our Father sent

E is for Everlasting life
That's what he always meant

A is for Adorable
Our Baby Jesus born

C is for the Christ we have
and

E is for Evermore.

Jennifer P. Lumley

Okay, Okay, It's Christmas

Okay, okay we always say
When Christmas comes around
We worry about the toys and gifts
But wait, don't make a sound

Just let me say a word to you
About the Christmas season
Stop fussing about the petty things
Let's get to know the reason

God up above looked down on earth
Upon His lovely nation
And deep down in His heart He knew
That they would need salvation

So down He sent His baby boy
His parents called Him Jesus
And from a lowly manger bare
Comes this strong power that frees us.

Welch's Glue

Courtney; nothing ordinary about this man.
People-person, good father, great son.
No ordinary man
Steel worker, youngest son, Church brother;
No ordinary man.
Comforter and adviser to nieces and nephews.
God's child, husband and…no ordinary man!

God gave us an inspiration in Courtney
Hope we've learned lessons from this extra-ordinary man
Inspired, encouraged, supported and became the Welch's glue.
No ordinary man.
God gave us His son Jesus
Certainly, no ordinary man!

The familiar road that we travel
Doesn't always take us home
Fret? No, not for this quintessential soul
For he did not roam.

All that he had he gave to you
All that he knew he taught us all
All he was just shone right through
All he's become is from God's call!

Rev. Clinton Glen is one of the coolest Ministers I have ever known. The children absolutely loved him and at end of year this 'rap' was an idea of a dedication to him. 'Rapping' was just getting popular.

Yo, Reverend Glen

Yo, Reverend Glen, you're the leader of the pack
We just wanna bring some memories back
Remember when we started we were all so shy?
Well now it's different and here is why
Between Mrs. Ojeda and Mrs. Hunt
We had to do some singing and get rid of the grunt
Listen congregation, it really wasn't easy
If you didn't wanna sing then you had to get busy
Doing something that you might really hate
You either do that or you come in late.

We had guest artists doing singing and dancing
We learned to socialize, we learned fraternizing
Then Miss Lumley would come in and say
"Okay young people, what you thinking today?"
We spoke to her well, we didn't hold back
She would give us an award or a pat on the back
She recognized each and every one of us
Knew what made us unique, so there was never a fuss

We had open discussions 'bout things that were related
To our everyday lives; I mean we even debated
'Bout fact and fiction, 'bout true and false
'Bout God and Jesus; even shopping malls
And so as it comes to the end of the year
We are saying this so you will hear
How we've lived so happily
I mean it's really cool, it's just like family.

We've celebrated birthdays and special occasions
We had a real cool time, now it's time for vacation
We wave goodbye, we bid you adieu
You'll see us next year and we'll see you too!

Jennifer P. Lumley

My Relationship with Christ

No man cometh to the Father, except through Jesus Christ
So my relationship with Him is always kept just right
A personal way in which to stay connected to the Word
My behavior therefore is dictated by my personal, loving Lord

Keep away from displeasure, for you are joined and intertwined
So hold on tightly and embrace this love for Christ so kind
Grasp tightly with your hand and heart with fervor and affection
Display gratitude at all times; you'll never lose your direction.

Little Candles

Little candles, little light
Making things look warm and bright
Little children, God's creation
Hoping for a peaceful nation.

A Tribute to Barbara M. Simpson

Barbara M. Simpson, a journalist of unparalleled qualities, wrote for the Jamaica Weekly Gleaner (NA Edition) for thirty one years before taking her writing skills to New York's CARIB News. An alumni of Excelsior College, Jamaica, she went on to join The British Army's Women's Royal Army Corps (WRAC) and was one of the confidential secretaries in the unit.

Any attempt to quantify the myriad of ways in which Barbara touched the lives of the many people that she knew, or any suggestion that may be made to qualify the love she had for her church and pastor, and all the persons with whom she made contact; any such attempt would be preposterous.

Barbara brought value to life and like the Goshen stone brought a kaleidoscope of colorful words to describe it. Goshen stones have those silver, bluish-grey, copper, rust and gold tones. Splendidly colorful!

The Goshen stone is one of high value and you could step right past it, because it is simply a stone. But the Goshen stone is a Micaschist, metamorphic, flat stone formed in the lower Devonian period, over 400 million years ago. When Barbara talked, you experienced history. She took you way back.

Goshen stones come in two forms: a common grade and a fine grade. Need one say more? Among its other uses, the finer quality Goshen stones are used to create stone art and pillars in homes and palaces. That to me represents Barbara, a rock in society, a stalwart with varied and artistic abilities. A person of excellence!

The face of the Jamaican Diaspora and the world at large has changed, but the beauty of this Goshen stone will always be remembered. Ever rest in peace WriterBabs!

The Life of a Good Soldier

A soldier once with sense of pride and total admiration
A writer without writer's cramp and sense of definition
A mother and grandmother too with steps perfectly ordered
A treasure and a bosom friend, this playful, valiant soldier
THE LIFE OF A GOOD SOLDIER MUST GO ON

Erect she stood and pensive would her countenance become
This polished queen, sometimes serene and other times just awesome
Her strength and fine intelligence no common speech revealed
A scribe she was and often showed how written words were sealed
THE LIFE OF A GOOD SOLDIER MUST GO ON

Bereft she was of worldly goods but never would she repine
She had no fears for all her cares belonged to the Divine
This journalist extraordinaire, evinced her love for church
Smiles of light within her eyes, glimpses of tranquil mirth
THE LIFE OF A GOOD SOLDIER MUST GO ON

Revelations in her writings, thoughts in articles nonpareil
Succinct description of fame and bliss or litany on life surreal
But those whose fate it was to suffer often did not understand
Why she ministered to them as scribe and lent a helping hand
THE LIFE OF A GOOD SOLDIER MUST GO ON

Her bravest self was not at war, nor on a battlefield
But nestled quietly in her bed, with God as her only shield
With discipline she crossed the spume to her God with pure delight
Soldier cease your worldly roles; close the window now, it's twilight.
THE LIFE OF A GOOD SOLDIER MUST GO ON.

Imaginary Ship

Upon the fluffiest cloud I sat in my imaginary ship
From there I saw magnificence, I'm glad I took the trip
The sun came up and shone upon the people down below
Investing in imperishables so kindness and love can grow

A fresh wind blew and then I saw a manifold of doves
A choir sang as new day dawned manifesting God's love
Variegated butterflies with beautiful wings unfurled
Flowers gave birth and fragrance filled the whole entire world

My ship now changed direction, unnaturally catapulted
By a sinister, unexpected wind, sequestered and insulted
Hypocrisy now all dressed up, pompous egos now parade
Idle tongues and darkness of mind are such a masquerade

I steered my ship back to its place where it originally sat
I like the white and fluffy clouds and that is simply that
I know Utopia is a place where we can sometimes be
An imaginary ship is all you need to take you there, you'll see

Section 4) LIFE

I wrote this in May 2004. See what Tolle's 'A New Earth' has to offer on the subject in 2008. You will be pleasantly surprised.

Tolerating Madness

Creativity expresses madness
That has been pent up in our mind's eye

Imagination and dreams
Come forth, but who are we to ask why?

Ideas accepted as society's norms
Take various times, eras and forms
When we're not shy

Practice they say makes perfect
Perfection I think is practical

ZERO tolerance is what I have for re-work,
Bye.

Jennifer P. Lumley

Weapons

Weapons, war, West Bank, worship
Persistent pushing, poll–bearing hypocrite
Destruction, obstruction, pollute a whole nation
Avarice, jealousy, malfunction of station
Station in life or rank behind father
Carries home body bags; now one less brother
Foolish, fearless fighting fits full this frame
Doggone it, give me the gall to call this a name.

Television, newspapers and all the others
Bear false news seven days for twenty four hours
Hope rises, fear falls, prayers go up
Another nineteen year old just bit the dust
Front-liner of course; seasoned ones wait around
Oh crap! Helicopter with seven just shot down
To love is such a damn hard thing to do
Let's end that, start loving and let it flow.

Congressmen have no children in the military
Education costs covered if you live as a dignitary
Ten thousand dollars: sounds good to poor Blacks
But what good is that with brains blown out in Iraq?
Just for trying to live good; for trying to get better
You end up far away looking for a mere letter
Let's get smart, let's not fight, put this in its frame
God damn it, I know this thing is a mere game.

Mind Shaper

Recruit the untrained minds
And teach them new disciplines

Wasted time and exploration
Of the unknown, will cause
Further curiosity into
Unnecessary trouble and the
Perfection of the art of doing
Nothing…endlessly.

An early start in the day, in the
Education and the whole life,
Shows vision, finds ways and means
Encourages action…perpetually.

Knows various non-traditional,
Novel practices, evokes a higher
Mental approach, sees the end,
Knows no obstacle, builds character
From new experiences and looks again
For another eighty six thousand four hundred seconds
To elaborate and stabilize
The generation coming forth
In preparation for a new day
And a different battle.

Jennifer P. Lumley

Won't Ever...Again

Freckles, curls, smile, soft hands
Yellow, boyish, glasses, not bland
Eat and drink and drive that's lost
Dinner, lotto, gas – no cost.

Ever had a dream return?
Ever, ever gotten burnt?
Ever dared to try again?
Ever know it's gonna rain?

Ever, ever, ever trust?
Ever knew it was a must?
Ever seen past turn to present?
Ever loved and then resent?

Ever watched him go right past?
Ever knew it wouldn't last?
Ever had the child within?
And watch and wake and feel it spin?

And then he goes away?

Almost Every Subject

A deep understanding of subjects
Is what the records show
It indicates to me therefore
That we should also know
The teachings and the writings
Of renowned historians and scientists
Works of Shakespeare or Sir Thomas Moore
Boccaccio and Cervantes

These unique individuals
Set good works in the making
Challenging viewpoints and skillful approach
Check out Sir Francis Bacon
Philosophy, Math and Science
Medicine, Poetry and Music
Gravity, Finance and Philosophy
Religion, Culture and Rhetoric.

Socrates, Plato and Aristotle
Hales and Plotinus as well
Saint Augustine and Machiavelli
All have so much to tell
Exposure to the finer arts
And simply reading a book
Strong dialogue and some knowledge
Brings a gradual, cultural outlook

Examine the literary movement
The Renaissance has carried
Dante, Erasmus, Hagel and Locke
Different views, desirously fancied
In Italy it all began
And spread throughout the world
And once the focus was on the men
But now it's on boys and girls

The pulse of these iconic folks
You feel in their books on logic
On government and integrity
Psychology as well as ethics
Politics and the theater
I'm naming just a few
Of the many subjects covered
On what these great men knew

Sublation, idealism and dialectics
Are worth more discussions these days
Aesthetics is due much more review
To give the proper praise
Read Spenser or some Chaucer
Take time to do so soon
Do so before some earthlings
Start inhabiting the moon.

Only Child

Four girls, two boys make six altogether
One young, bright-eyed woman, Mamie, the mother
But somewhere, somehow in her life
There's one who feels like an only child

The only child born at home and delivered
By a midwife, Granny Darlin'; all old and withered
Named by an Aunt because of the circumstances
"Faith" exercised and nothing left to chances

The only child born with blondish hair
The only child after two whose skin was fair
The only child who spent time with Papa and his Spanish
The only child whose last name made her feel "one-ish"

The only child who left school and without assistance
Pursued her career and met much resistance
The only child who migrated to the Metropolis, New York
Doing for herself the work of the stork

The only child that had two or three jobs at a time
The only child that wore anything and still looked just fine
Sought good education for herself and her child
Soccer matches, violin performances also took time

In her pain her doctors said she had extra ribs
No wonder she's different from the rest of her sibs
At seventeen suffered with epileptic seizures
What animal is this, what a wicked creature?

Only love she bestows on sisters and brothers
On her nephews and nieces and all of the others
The aunts and grand-aunts and uncles to count
Grand-uncles all shower her with love from a fount

Cousins and in-laws and friends far and near
Class mates and school mates and church friends so dear
Value her love and she cherishes them so
Teachers remember and now that we know

She only, only she used to think she was
An Only Child.

Green Teeth

Running around at maximum speed
Chomping and eating all slimy with greed
Enjoying the feast of stinking, rotten decay
Making sure that there's no one around in its way

The white of its eyes, are all bloodshot and red
This maniacal, evil, overweight, half-dead
Green teethed, scaly skinned, foul parasite
Will eat you all up with chomps and bites

Arm yourself, stay away, it will bring you harm
Doing right does not help, don't turn on your charm
Just resist, slip away, run as fast as you can
It's unhealthy to stay in this dark dungeon

It has so many names, you wonder and ponder
Filthy, unwholesome, brutish, old liar
Insensitive, unconscionable, ruthless but reliable
The evils of the credit cards are undeniable.

When you sometimes cannot see the light, but know you are in a perpetual tunnel, remember that someone, somewhere has faith in you.

Fail?

You cannot fail. You were not born to fail
You have never failed
Is this a new trend?
Do you have a new friend?
I don't suspect so
I am, as a matter of fact, quite sure.

I'm quite grateful indeed
For the high level of commitment
And the support that you have given me
New furniture for my arrival
Curtains and cushions bright
A new car in which to drive
And bright fluorescent light

Splendid fresh arrivals from the grocery store
You need a committee to meet you at the door
Fail? Who dares to draw that conclusion?
I recognize your sacrifices. What's the confusion?

More Than A Million Ways To Walk

Slippers, Thongs and Sandals, Flip-flops, Wedges and Booties
Some Cowboy Boots and Mary-Janes and Moccasins are cuties
They're trendy and refreshing especially Baby Heels
Or Blue Suede Shoes and Platforms and those for climbing trees

There are Bowling, Combat, Hiking Boots, Waders and Hush Puppies
Mules and Monks and Lace-up Shoes, Penny Loafers for the Yuppies
School Shoes, Tap and Ballet Shoes are sold wholesale and retail
The Peep Toe, Stomps and Strappies do require a lot of detail

The cushioned, sequined Ankle Wraps made of shiny, patent leather
Are different from those Wellingtons that help you brave bad weather
Sneakers, Trainers, Trotters, Flats offer some amount of comfort
The crisp new feel of Kitten Heels makes me suspect they're imports

Snow Boots, Ski Boots, Derby Boots, rugged Football and Soccer Cleats
Go-Go, Kinky and Sculptured Boots are all made for women's pretty feet
Glittery, cheap, man-made, fun shoes, Toeless, Converse and Jellies
Sockdals, House Shoes, Hi-Tops and Crocs worn mainly watching tellies

Oxfords, T-Straps and Galoshes cannot be classified as the same
Then Golf Shoes and Orthopedics would fall under a common name
There are distinctive differences between Costume and demure
Sometimes hardly noticeable but with Espadrilles you're sure

Funky Flower-Pot Sole Shoes or formal Three-Cun Lilies
Or Straw Sandals and Martial Arts and Stitch-Soles are for Chinese
The very merry Ankle Straps or sweet, carefree Bunny Slippers
The soft, plush High Heels are no match for casual Brothel Creepers

Jennifer P. Lumley

Dutch Wooden Shoes and Japanese Getas or those that are called Zaris
Or pretty Khassa Indian Shoes and shoes designed for the safaris
Tatami Sandals, Nursing Shoes, racy Pumps are versatile
Expensive Tennis Shoes you bet, will always be in style

Of leather Boots and plastic Uggs or Dream Heels or Puff Slippers
Or chic Snakeskins, embroidered Clogs, I think I will just differ
Blue Boot for those eleven steps can cause some amount of stir
Worse would be Motorcyclers trimmed with sparkles and with fur

Swim-fins are classified as shoes I really don't know how
But Sheepskin softens all your steps and doesn't cause a row
Sleek Skating Shoes, seductive Sling Backs, Open Toes galore
Intriguing Slip-Ons will cause a stare; eye catching that's for sure

When you decide to wear Cupid's Shoes, a pedicure will enhance it
They're slight, seductive and full of style; step carefully, don't chance it
You will be called flirtatious, they'll say you have sex appeal
Indeed you are simply a jet-setter with Stilettos nonpareil

Those curvy calves are delicate and show off your finesse
Your bold new moves and expensive shoes are exciting at best
Exquisite, vibrant silhouette are the very best obtainable
Stilettos always steal the show, on the floor and on the table

Stilettos look intelligent, provocative and coquettish
Will cause political espionage, this love for shoes, this fetish
There are a million types of shoes some of which you will endorse
But the personality of sexy Stilettos becomes par for the course

Now after you have walked and stepped and sauntered on the streets
Strolled in the grass, hopped in the shower or ran over to the beach
Emancipate your toes at last, make your day complete
You'll soon discover, you and your lover, there's nothing like bare feet.

eMerle

Has anyone told you that you were sweet?
Has someone said they think you're neat?
Did they say something really kind?
You see these are the ties that bind

Dear Merle you are dependable
You e-mails are always remarkable
You don't compete to bring a smile
Yours are all together in a file

And on the day I have no sun
You are the one that brings the fun
From "Looking for men" to "Picking flowers"
I laugh so hard, I cry in showers

So Merle, when you get another chance
Look over your shoulders, take a glance
I won't be there to laugh with you a lot
I'll be waiting on his end to see what e-mails I got.

Jennifer P. Lumley

Circuit Breaker

Approaching the smooth darkness,
I searched for the area most likely
To produce sensitivity, slight shock.
This was not my first time, but
This was my first big one.
Apprehension filled me as I moved
Around the area almost aimlessly, not knowing.
It is real, it is gonna pay me good
I'm hardly able to inhale enough air
To catch breath and to fill my lungs
Before it's time again for me to
Keep moving to the pace of my racing heart.

Deafening silence; stiff, hard darkness
Dripping; no, more like oozing on my lips
From a long black pipe; unfamiliar, yet familiar
I had done this once before
Different from the ones I know.
Uncontrollable breathlessness.
Then I felt the hole, tense and locked
As though frightened by the world of
Deep, solid, lonely, strange darkness.
Membrane surrounding the entry passage
Was like a well woven spider's web.

I have to get in there and change the form
Opposites attract, negative and positive connect
And finally, almost afraid, scared and tired
I told him to try it. "Put it on I said
It's the only way to do this".
CLICK!
He flicked the switch and they all saw me
Experiencing this mini earthquake, shuddering;
And I had come, to fix the bank's circuit breaker.

Personal Preference

Confirmation, "Yes, I want to attend"
Cancellation, family matters I must amend
Confusion thinking it's a black tie affair
Conclusion: We all must be there

Linda, Carol, Roz, Jennifer and the whole gang
Make PPI at the Raddisson a great big shibbang
Lisa's Lightening Force shining bright
Tami Cohen watches us take special flight

The only thing I see on the faces of all
Is not knowing if they'll have a ball
For sure, however, the ambiance that's set
So hosts and guests have no reason to fret

There are so many guests but no more seats
But excitement builds when the "bunny hop' beats
We sing and we talk and we greet and we smile
Eating's good, raffle's great but the auction's gone wild.

Jennifer P. Lumley

Who Wants This Life?

When life won't let up, always casting you down
When life won't let up and you've got to leave town
When life messes up and you can't find a job
When life messes up and you run into a sob

When life becomes really messed up and down
'Cause the son of a gun will not leave town
He announces quite publicly you are "only a friend"
Privately, however, he wants to use you to the end

When life won't let up and you try to run away
When hopes become dashed because you've gone astray
Now you're looking for love and it has you cast down
You don't know it will find you so you are going around

In circles so big, unfamiliar and strange
In places a cat or a dog would get mange
When transparency won't become a uniform
So no one can see you in your personal storm

When life gets you wet then dries you to the bone
When life gets you fat, then thin, meager and gaunt
When life speeds you up then suddenly slows down
Then it's now quite apparent that you have reached way down

When life spreads you thin all over the place
When life loses rhythm and you lose your pace
When life deals a deck that you don't want to play
Then life may have won, but you won't delay

New faces may help, new surroundings may last
Life teases again and starts moving fast
New choices to make from a different menu
Different day, same crap, just a whole new venue

When life presents challenges from out of this world
No one ever heard of, just you and the little girl
And twenty years later you feel you've succeeded
In making her into what she just needed

Up comes the jackal from out of nowhere
Haunting your dreams and setting his snare
From the entrails of hell, this damn son of a bitch
Appears and wreaks havoc, havoc you never wished

Baby girl seems grown now, but little does she know
What caused the premature furrows in my brow
How much pain he has caused, how much venom he's carried
It continued from the very Saturday we got married

When life won't let up and won't give you a break
When life won't let up and behaves like a snake
When life won't let up and you get a real sting
And life lets you down loudly with a bang and a ring

So life won't let up, but you know just what?
LIFE is not in charge, we all know that
So how did it manage to get you cast down?
Deprived you of a job and let you leave town?

Jennifer P. Lumley

Dashed hopes, haunted dreams and let you run away?
Lost your friends, tested sanity and let you go astray?
How was it that nothing could take full control?
Gave love away for nothing, but almost sold your soul

When you take control, make up your mind at long last
That God is the only one you can really trust
That God is the answer, the key and the Master
That God is the light, He'll remove dark disaster

You must pray and ask for His help like a friend
You must give Him your troubles, give Him, not lend
You must believe He will do it, no doubt at all
You must look for the answer like in a shopping mall

You know it's there, you haven't seen it yet
Ask Him some more, ask Him, don't fret
Live victoriously, take the challenge, trust Him my dear
Claim the storehouse of blessings He has up there

Smile and be happy and don't get annoyed
Answer is coming, for He has not toyed
You are far too important for Him to forget
A star in His eye, a precious gem you can bet

So true to His word, never lets you down
A feather in His cap, a jewel in His crown
Now you feel lighter, your burdens are gone
Your strong belief in God is second to none

Shop around for more blessings, don't forget to say thanks
This is your day of victory, God does not play pranks
Help yourself to a sigh of relief and smile once again
It is lighter than burdens and sure better than pain

Share love with someone, tell them of God
How good He can be, if given a chance
Shine sunshine, shine. Take gloom away
It's my day, it's my day, it's my day, Oh yeah!!!

Thursday's Child

So I walked onto the beach
Felt like a woman unleashed
Trying to absorb the last bit of sun
My top needed color and so did my bun
Leaving already? Want me to stay?
Question answering question; it's cool it's Thursday

The knock on the door by the sweet chambermaid
Awakened my soul, brought clarity to my head
Hurriedly but carefully I washed, bathed and dressed
With lotion and oils my sweet body I caressed
Frantically chasing around town I found out
Businesses close early; nothing to worry about

Back to the drawing board; he said he would stay
But I knew I'd be returning to the USA
On the first day of JazzFest, I froze my tail off
White cargo pants, pink off-the-shoulder blouse, soft
The same beach towel I left on the back seat
Came to my rescue and became my "heat"

There is nothing that I've ever known
That could have taken away that frown
And quickly turn it into a smile
After teeth chattered for many a mile
I offered gum as I traveled on the bus
"A three pack it looks like; looks like condoms to us"
Three English girls busted out in such laughter
Echoing friendship and sisterhood thereafter.

My Uncle Allan

The peaceful, silent closing
Of the door of this life
Has left a measure of sincere grief
And joy, visibly and profoundly
Felt by those with whom he had any contact

I charge any or all of you today
To be as self-sacrificing as
Allan Neil Stone.
The generous instincts of this fine man
Will be missed.

Four Fives

Five years ago I was a slave

Five years later a mere knave

Five times redone my resumé

Five years later, do you think I'll stay?

So now?

Korwaatch and I

9:20 comes and you think you are present
With a smile you bid her good morning
She's gonna 'pink' you, not mark you absent
For there's no uniform and you're yawning.

10 o'clock is here and you beg for a break
Don't talk to her about it
She'll ignore you till you have a heart ache
Or sit with your mouth and just pout it

Surprise, surprise, she throws a test
She knows just what we are doing
We look intelligent at best
But just who do we think we're fooling

That wise old owl she bears a grin
She makes you start to ponder
Conversation starts 'bout Jim and Lynn
You think 'I've failed, no wonder'

It's five to one, she's called your name
You think you're gonna make it
You run like hell, this ain't no game
And with Korwaatch you just can't fake it

So now a few people are missing
For Korwaatch has stuck to the rule
They're probably happily shopping
Don't feel sorry for them! Who's the fool?

Hi Miss Korwaatch, hi Gilma, hi everyone
She knows this sign-in sheet is Augie's
He barely gets an answer from anyone
In truth this guy is all three stooges

Bye Carwash! Bye Penelope
You now know it's 2 O'clock
Will that day come when finally
Penelope will say Korwaatch?

There's liquid bleach, there's powder too
Which of the two is stronger?
No you don't have to taste it, that's not true
Don't you want to live much longer?

Twenty volume peroxide, polypeptide bonds
Ammonium Thioglycolate
I know she knows their purpose and all
But will she ever say them straight

She walks around the room at no steady pace
Don't be too close when she talks
She's wondering why you made the funny face
Finds out it's an earache and laughs

The left side of the classroom
Is usually a riot
But on the right where Class H isn't
It's awfully, I mean awfully quiet

This is Class I as I list them
It's not necessarily true
But this is how I saw us
So really it's my view

Jennifer P. Lumley

Charlene is our long-haired lady
She has long nails too
Olga is our time keeper
And I mean that through and through

Danielle is our Ja-Merican
Hates shopping with her mother
Wears her jewelry well though
That's why she loves 'the brother'

Gilma is our 'hola, que pasa'
She hails from Columbia
Elena is our 'Como esta'
Bears the flag of Ecuador

Maria is our little girl
Sandra is super quiet
Frances is undecided
As to her latest hairstyle and diet

And then there is Jozfin, last on the list
Habibi was really shy
Don't call her sharmuta, she'll be ticked
And of that I tell you no lie

She's a fine kid from Iran you know
With great upbringing too
But now she's in America
She can do what she wants to do

Mrs. Korwaatch we had so much fun
Right here in room number four
Maybe one day we'll come back to visit
If not we'll just peek through the door.

Kill that Headache

It will soon be five days now, since I got this headache so severe
It throbs in the center if my head and beats behind my ears
My eyes have also been affected; I cannot bear to see the light
Incandescent or fluorescent, or radiance of dawn seems too bright

I wonder if I stayed too hungry and was famished for much too long
Or if I ate something in my meals, that for my system was just wrong
Those delicious plantain chips on Thursday or Fridays salt fish dinner
Or the very fragrant potpourri at the viewing in the funeral parlour

Tossing and turning in bed on Saturday night resulted in sleep deprivation
So the very few hours of sleep that I got, sure did not help the situation
Then up and early to church on Sunday, for my special ordination service
Followed by rushing to make photocopies and racing to my Mom's place

The words that I hear sound muffled, my voice is now feeling quite raspy
So my throat is hoarse and when I cough my eyes get all red and watery
Oh me, oh my what must I do, what other remedies should I try
I've eaten, I've slept, I've rested and I've turned off all the lights

My cerebellum feels as though I had been picked up and badly shaken
Like things haven't settled down just yet, or I had been rudely awakened
But I think I had a little strawberry drink that didn't sit well with my palate
It 's label said 'light' and I realized this sweetener could put me in a casket

I've tried to drink a lot of water attempting to flush out my system
I am also carefully reading my labels making sure to regain my rhythm
I've tried some pain killers and I've made an ice pack for my forehead
But nothing worked until I drank my bowl of hot, cornmeal porridge!

Jennifer P. Lumley

Make It Your Home

King and queen live in a palace, a minister in a manse
Fine horses in their stables, that is where they prance
Your place of abode's your haven, to you it has its worth
Home is always where you go, it's where you will find comfort

The Aborigine's home is a humpy, of that we can agree
And Native American Indians have a wigwam or a teepee
The nobles in their castles live ostentatiously well
The snail across the pathway does just fine in its shell

The beaver goes to its lodge, the lion to its peaceful den
Birdy settles quietly in a nest, piggy has a sty or a pen
A coop is for the chicken, a web is home to a spider
Prisoner's home is called a cell, he must wish it were wider

The tiger and the fox we know both call their home a lair
Igloos are for the Eskimos and the den is for the bear
Owls are found in barns or trees and in a fold are the sheep
Lumberjacks have log-cabins from a hard day's work they'll sleep

When it's tranquility you seek or you simply want to flourish
Food for both body and mind, go home you will get nourished
Soldiers' barracks or dog's kennel or a little hole for a mouse
Your place of abode's your haven, it's your home, it is your house.

Section 5) NATURE

Nature Haiku

Green caterpillars
Small trees in radiant bloom
Summer breeze gently blows

Shimmering bright lights
Alive at home with presents
Dead tree marks new life

River rushes fast
Footsteps change its direction
Wet feet are now happy

Naked leafless tree
Harsh winter winds keep blowing
Summoning the spring

Country road and trees
Singing birds and butterflies
Make long journey short

White frost on windshield
Images of cold rhythm
Autumn comes again

Section 6) PRAYERS & MEDITATION

Prayer for UTech Alumnae Awards Ceremony

Most high God, we thank and praise you for your presence here tonight. Abide with us as we take this journey together. We thank you for having taken us thus far and we pray that as the program progresses, we will remember to treasure our past, find joy in the present and great hope for the future.

Eternal God, continue to love us, have mercy upon us and show us your way. You, dear God are the omnipotent. Help us to understand that without a name, a title or an occupation, we have still been made into eternal living beings, created in unconditional love, by God.

Father we are grateful for the presence of everyone here tonight. We are particularly thankful for those who have traveled from far, for those who have shown unwavering support for the college and for those who have been outstanding examples from whom we can glean lessons of excellence.

We pray that this Awards Banquet tonight, will be one of many more successful ones to come. Bless the hearts and minds that planned this function to its entirety. We ask, also God that you will bless the meal that we will consume later. Bless the hands that prepared it. We pray for the nourishment of our bodies and the replenishment of our strength.

In Jesus' name and for His sake we pray.

Amen.

Jennifer P. Lumley

Standing Steadfast in God's Word

Have you ever felt so resolutely bound to do something, wrong or right, despite the consequences that you will have to face later? As children sometimes we think we must have a certain toy, if not we will throw a temper tantrum or just ask the other parent or an aunt or an uncle. We find ways to get what we want.

As adults, we sometimes have different needs and become creative in obtaining and satisfying those needs; that new house or car… and we are willing to sacrifice purchasing the new suit or dress that we want so badly…and, oh and the shoes, the restaurants. We attend fewer social functions and actually survive!!! We would work overtime, even though the taxes are greater on overtime pay, but we find the means by which we will be able to achieve our desired goal. We even tithe less than we should, if you know what I mean. God does!!!

In the spiritual realm, there are those folks who stand steadfast in God's word and will not waver. They find a way to worship, to pray, to spread good news and allow God's work to be constantly present in their lives. They have faith and show mercy. They know no other way and nothing can cause them to be different. The weather won't stop them from choir practice or prayer meeting or lending a helping hand in some other area that may need it.

Yes, there are such people…in this world, now, standing steadfast in the Lord and His holy works.

According to the Concise Oxford English Dictionary (11th Edition), the definition of STEADFAST is: "resolutely or dutifully firm and unwavering". Are you such a person? Do you know such a person?

Have you ever been in close contact with him/her? Does it feel like it's contagious or catching? Did you pass him/her by or just thought he/she was a fanatic? Or do you try to undermine the efforts of this person, doing God's work?

The Psalmist says in Chapter 119v76 "Let Your steadfast love become my comfort according to Your promise to Your servant." The Psalmist shows faith and puts it into action by believing, and he recognizes the true love of God.

Certainly you have experienced God's love and compassion. There is a sweetness about God's love that makes you crave for more; it is like none other. There is an abundance of God's love that is not burdensome. There a presence of God's love that keeps you constant company. There is a newness about God's love that is refreshing. These are only some of the characteristics of God's love that people can't wait to get more of.

One of the main reasons, the experience of God's love is so wonderful, is simply that it is STEADFAST. It is unwavering; God's love is so great that it cannot be weighed or measured. Save your tape measures and yard sticks. Put away the scales and only let God's love become your comfort. "Oh that my ways were steadfast in obeying Your decrees", Your laws, Your goodness for me." God's love does not submit itself to measurement. Can you imagine??? God's goodness is out of this world and beyond.

Psalm 19 v13 says "For sin will have no dominion over you, since you are not under (man's) law, but under (God's) grace.

Isaiah 26v3 refers to standing steadfast. It says "You will keep in perfect peace, him whose mind is STEADFAST because he trusts You.

In other words, because we have put our trust in God and not placed our confidence in man, we will live in peace. (Psalm 118v9)

Ps 112v7 "He will have no fear of bad news; his heart is steadfast trusting the Lord." God always finds a way to protect His own…it is almost **_by any means necessary._**

If you know of God, you know that His love is unwavering. You know that He is resolutely and dutifully firm in making sure that you are loved. He does not have to save or sacrifice in one area of your life to show you love in another, like we do when we need that new car or the new house. You don't have to throw a temper tantrum to find God's love or get His attention. You will not be deprived of anything when you allow God to love you. His love abounds, it surrounds and He is always to be praised.

Let us take a look at Ps 57v7; it reads "My heart is steadfast, O God my heart is steadfast; I will sing and make music." When you feel God's unconditional love, you make others become curious. Why the smile? Things are always perfect for him/her; she always sings or hums; he whistles a happy tune; it's because of his/her skin tone; they came from a different family background than ours.

No my friend. We are from the family of God and as long as we know God and recognize God's love and we love Him in return, nothing is too hard. No task impossible, no manager or employee to crude to get along with, no neighbor too strange to understand, no child too recalcitrant to return to the fold, no disease so unknown that it cannot be healed.

Dig your heels in and roll up your sleeves. There is work to be done as long as you have a pulse! God gives you 86,400 seconds everyday. Spend every moment being happy even when you don't understand. That is work. Lay your troubles to rest in His hands when they are beyond you. That is an arduous task. Smile and do not do what people expect you to do when they cut you off in traffic. That is almost unheard of!!! Redo the test you failed and see if you may not graduate with honors rather than just barely making it. That is very difficult.

Claiming the storehouse of victory that God has in store for you is work; it is yours for free, but you must remember to go get it. You have to be STEADFAST, faithful and upright. God's promise of salvation awaits you while He preserves your life.

In closing let me say what Peter said in 1Peter 5v10.
"And the God of all grace, who called you to his eternal glory in Christ, after you have suffered a little while, will Himself restore you and make you strong and steadfast".

Amen.

Offertory Prayer

Almighty and eternal Father, we come before Thee with our monetary offering – an offering.

We know is not enough to thank you for the blessings you have bestowed upon us daily.

The blessing of brotherhood and peace in our immediate surroundings.

Help us to continue to spread the peace, the love, the joy and the hope within us to our friends and neighbors.

Help us to survive as friends and not fight as fools.
We ask that you accept this token of an offering in Jesus' name. Amen.

Youth Offering Prayers

Dearest Lord and Most heavenly Father, we thank You for this beautiful day.

We thank You for Your love and protection.

You have watched over our ways, and in love, known each and every one of us.

Lift up those of us that are put down by poverty, crime and injustice.

Help us to love our neighbors as ourselves, even when it's hard.

Please accept this humble offering Dear God, as a token of our love. In Jesus' name we pray.

Amen.

Prayer

Heavenly Father, we thank You for all that You have provided for us – good health, strength, food shelter and clothing, friends, family and loved ones.

Dear God we praise You for Your Almighty foresight and preparation for past generations, this present one and the many more to come. Only You know all that burdens our hearts and minds and only You can give us any kind of relief.

Enrich our spirits dear God. Help us to find strength in these trying days. Guide us, we beseech You, through this maze of torment and distress. Allow us to rethink any unkind or evil thoughts. Search us and cleanse us from anything unclean. Deliver to us a guiding light that will lead us in the straight and narrow way to heaven's doors and help us to appreciate every day, one at a time.

Stay with us dear God and help us to be rational, helpful, understanding and positive. Only You are God; only You are dependable. Deliver us from misery and help us to bear our burdens. Make them lighter Dear God. We believe and we claim that which You have promised. All these things we ask in the precious name of Your son Jesus and for His sake we pray.

Amen.

God is...

The newborn babe and the grey beard sage…both made in the image and likeness of God. They have the light of hope and a ray of peace within. They have form that you can touch and life that you can experience. That's who God is.

God is at the root of every tree and flower; present at the flowering of every bloom, the most beautiful of which shows its face from the crack in a rock, high and damp with moisture. That's just how God is.

God's presence is in the rippling of the shallow brook and the rhythm of the ocean's waves; never missing the perfect formation of a soft evening sunset or smashing hard the refractions against the waters in mid-Summer. God is the gentle breeze and the threatening storm winds; the morning dew and the thunderous rains; the fragrance of jasmine and the unpredictable design of each snowflake. That's what God does.

Green foliage on a mountain top, evidenced as blue; hibernating bears that wake up from a dormancy; elephants and ants show life – a presence all their own; strangely different but God's way. Toads and lemmings are a splendor because they are God's creatures. Fresh air in excess. The rainbow – a promise. This is some of what God gives.

God is the changing of the seasons, the renewal of energy, the magnificence of the great sequoia, the burnished red and gold leaves before they fall and decorate the playground for squirrels and children, in this ever moving universe.

God is in mother earth, teaching creativity, training mind-shapers and expressing talents in dancers and poets. Laughing. God's expansive, immeasurable love speaks quietly so you will hear and shouts loudly so you will listen.

God is alpha and omega. Pure beauty. God is light. God is love. God is…

Section 7) BRAWTA

Introduction to Brawta

The original essence of what forms or shapes a person (ethos) especially Jamaicans, is deeply rooted in the diverse, learned, shared behaviors (cultures) that existed, largely as a result of colonialism and slavery, in our pretty little island, Jamaica. Thus the strong presence, coexistence and "newness" of a people from the African continent, China, France, Germany, Great Britain, India, Italy, Lebanon, Portugal, Spain, Syria and a smaller population of Jews and other immigrants from various countries. Of course, we can't forget the Native Arawak, Carib and Taino Indians who thrived healthily on this island paradise, way before colonialism.

It is, therefore, no accident that the island's motto is "Out of many one people", nor is it surprising that a unique language emerged. Patois, a rich Afro-Euro-Indo-Caribbean, non-documented language whose art form evolves daily, provides a kaleidoscope of poignant expressions and rich exhilarations for every single thing on earth!

Experience a taste of Jamaica! Dare to read BRAWTA.

Greetings

Yeow
Yagga yow
Star
Hail up, mi bredren
Whaapen man, lang time
Yes Iya
Seen
Yeah Man. So 'ow tings
Bway, yuh wah si, nutten nah gwaan fi mi, yuh nah noe
Mi noe man
Seen, a so it go, yeah man
Yhu seet
Eee hi
Hey, yow. Cho!
Yuh na 'now man
Who
Wha'?
Seet deh
Mi ah tell yuh,
Den nuh suh,
Ah just so it go
Ya man
Everytime,
True
Chu chu
Irie den
Seen,
Yussimme doe
A suh it go man
Yush
Easy Nuh
Wan luv

Poised and Positioned

Ah waiting to turn the corner one day
And run right into him
'Cause a just can't get the gall up yet
To say hello without a grin

A nice sophisticated smile
That tells a lot about me
How well raised and trained I was
Finga' cock up drinking tea

But ah fraid say if him say hello
I might freeze and not respond
Ah mighta talk and start to speak
Den soun' like a real, dumb blonde

What I'm feeling is quite natural
I'm not afraid you see
But why the dickens I want to talk to him
And him don't even notice me?

Why the dundus bwoy rounna front desk
Nuh carry him argument elsewhere?
And the very black one round the corner
Nuh go fine himself a career?

Fi dem lines cyan rough you see
An' some mek you well waan laugh
Is like fi dem lyrics nah run out
Soun' like a pig in a trough

His skin reminds me of velvet
It's olive and so smooth
Him dress so good and always match
His presence puts you in a good mood

One day, one day, one outta seven
A gwine fine mi self a way
Fi invite 'im to church, something like dat
An' see what he would say

Then him mighta waan invite me to club
Then what would the decision be?
The church, the club, the club, the church
But what a calamity!!!

Well with my well-rounded background
We might as well do both
You have to know when and how to flex
In moderation, not overdose

So if it's a pious girl he wants
I will be there to deliver
And if is a rump-riding, dancehall style him chose
A gwine run and wind like a river!!!

Anyway, mi gawn, di phone credit run out
A de pon a special mission
Look like him coming roun di bend
So mi haffi tek up position....

Aunt Gloria's Thoughts on Monica

Manica, Manica bway
Is a good ting seh mi come
Manica, wat a jai
Yu fix mi frak
Wid two nice packet
Yuh sew so good
A want a jacket
An anadda outa-awda pants
Fi wear weh mi live
Put Canada people inna trance
Dem nevva see dissa side a mi yet
Mi singin' group wudda mus staat fret

Whoa! Manica Lewise gal
Yu fi see fi mi nephew Sal
A husband lakka him yu shudda fine
Gi yu likkle bit a peace o' mind
Wid di whole host a pickney way yuh gat
Tappy nize ya ooman, tap and mek mi chat
Yuh special; mi really glad mi meet you!
Y' hear?

Jennifer P. Lumley

Hot Air

Pscheow! It's time to go man, what is keeping up the bus?
Just one more deggay-deggay person causing such a fuss

The flight package did not say that we have to wait for him
On a day like today after a plane delay, it seems such a sin

One fooley-fooley ooman inna wan funny yellow dress
Wid fi her own plane problem and now dis ya bus mess

It's been quite a long while since I came here though
My husband died and I never know

That I would stay so long before returning,
Now my brother passed, what a mourning

But he lived a long full life and I thank God for him.
Lawd, a weh di bway deh man? This is seriously grim!

From The Eyes of the Blind

So 'ow else yuh gwine know
Seh di man really love yuh
If yuh nuh mek 'im lick yuh sometime
An nuh badda say nuttin'?

Yuh cyaan mek ooman get bad name
Wid behavia lakka dat
Yuh haffi hold on tight pon di baby
Wen yuh a get yuh bax!

Mek man come home to a strang ooman
An' nuh haffi go outta street
Go strut him stuff or nuh come home
Caa smaddy else si seh 'im sweet

Hole yuh lick and tek yuh slap
Nuh coob up lakka pigeon
Tighten yuh jawbone wen 'im come een
Show di man seh yuh have some vision

A nuh every man know 'ow fi treat ladies good
Yu haffi keep one wen 'im come 'roun
A tree baby father mi go choo
Before mi fine one wa cudda lick mi dung

When yuh open yuh eye fram dung a grung
An' look pon 'im well-pressed pants seam
Look pon di tall, strong man God mek
Dis 'ansome man of my dreams.

Obeah Stall

I nevva know seh obeah come
Inna summuch shape an size
Till when ah move go Kingston
I was shocked and most surprised

I see mi neighbor feed har chicken
Wid a can of mix–up sumting
An wen dem ready fi lay dem egg
Set good, it look like a pumpkin

Di adda neighba seh she nuh stap ya suh
An now mi staat to believe
Jus' fi wash some dish an tun dem down
Di pipe wata haffi run choo sieve

When she come home from work a evening time
Yu wouldda nevva guess wah she a do
Before she cyan enter fi her yard gate
She spin har roll an staat to moo

But she nat alone in Kingston
She nat alone at all
People go all a market
Fi set up dem obeah stall

Dem have every kinda flava
Any calla weh yuh can fine
Obeah come fi every single ting
Stap drink, past test and read mind

Yuh want get yuh young son outta jail
Or gi pretty gal fassy foot
Maas Joe upstairs, hold on pon di rail
'Im wi tell yuh wa fi duh

Obeah fi mek yuh sing loud inna choir
Or mek yuh clothes fit yuh right
Obeah fi get family a 'Merica
Fi staat to fuss an fight

Obeah fi mek yuh dumpling swell
An full up di whole pat
De kine a obeah wah mek people love yuh
Although yuh so big an fat

Di kind fi mek yuh lose weight
One fi mek yuh win di lattery
Obeah fi mek judge overrule
Charge 'gainst yuh fi assault an battery

Yuh waan write nice, waan marry rich?
Waan personality and sex appeal?
Waan good job, stay good lookin?
Mek me tell yuh di real deal

Yuh tink mi a charge yuh a fartune
Mek me tell yuh di plain truth
Yuh might get vex but wi a fren
Just listen to mi now, nuh shoot

Yuh see Massa God weh up deh so
A Him yuh fi go worship
Dash way di piece a ugly claat
Wah Maas Joe say a special 'kerchief

Stop crow so soon a mawnin time
Like seh yuh a some rooster
Tap gi Joe money fi foolishness
An try fine God the Master

Di life-size cyadboad man a yuh door
Nah attrack no man fi marriage
Pig inna pen wid spoon all bout
Nah mek dem nyam hat parridge

Go down pon yuh knee and talk to God
No matter how bad He can stand it
God will grant you your wishes
Joe cyaan do it fi yuh; Joe a BANDIT!!!

Miss Rabby Son

Oonu see Miss Rabby good-good son
Wah go a callege an' come back
A walk pon street den staat to run
An hap aan pon bike back?

Look like di bway deh mad to mi
Ah so mi feel right now
But who fi tell jus wah deh gwaan
Afta four years wut a snow

Ah some serious cold deh a 'Merica
Wi drive yuh out a yuh mind
Mi nuh surprise di bway de act so
A talk loud and a mek some sign

But a look mi look good de adda day
A misself mi haffi blame
Bax front! nuh cell phone inna im ays
Mi nearly get misself a name!!!

Jennifer P. Lumley

Cologne de'Onion

Yuh constitution strang missis
Gad bless yuh and dat deh man
I don't know if yuh don't smell
Him cologne de'Onion

Di man mout full a ratten teet
An every minute 'im waan fi kiss
Mek sure yuh get yuh tetnus shat
Jus in case wan day 'im miss

Den dat deh mustache pon 'im face
Wah curl up like two ess
Look like it have inhabitants
An di beard is jus a mess

'Im shut neck brown fa 'im have ring 'roun
Di calla and di sleeve
Dress nuh cockroach and step inna coach
'Im is a prince is wat 'im believe

One evening 'im pass mi dung a road
Look sharp and tink 'im sweet
What a ting when di brute come close to mi
Smell like some stale season meat

Mi eyes staat burn; dat a onion
Skellion an thyme mek mi sneeze
But the other unidentifiables
Mek mi stiffen like mi freeze!

What's In A Name

Mi nuh name Ann-Marie, Beverly or Constance
Sonia, Shirley or Teresa
Precious, Donna, Marcia or Puncie
My name is MONA LISA

You tink seh wid such a nice nice name
Dem wouldda put mi pickcha pon a wall
An bring nuff gifts based pon mi name
But a nuh so at all

All Betty, Susan, Jean and Winsome
'Ave dem birthday party every year
An mi happy fi go if dem invite mi
Aldoh mi nuh tink say it fair

When Heather family go pon picnic
And Lorraine gone to tek dance classes
Karen, Monique and Sharon a play
Mona Lisa a wash plates and glasses

Mi sing sometime till mi tune run out
Mi hum so till mi staat get tyad
Mi thoughts cyaan come outta mi mouth
Believe mi for mi a nuh liad

Lorna, Angela, Pamela and Maud
Gloria, Marilyn, Lucy or Grace
Audrey, Sandra, Louise or Gwen
Barbara and Alice have a place

Ah wanda why some parents don't tek time out
Fi gi dem children a good name
Nuh no funny name wah gi yuh tie tongue
Nor wah mek yuh pickney look shame

Ah wanda if dem ever tink for a while
Seh children could gain de right
Fi re-name dem parents after certain age
It wouldda drive dem into fright

Dem wouldda give careful consideration
To the task of naming dem children
And after much deliberation
We would all have a proper name

Nuttin dat's too hard fi spell
Or fi read or fi pronounce
Rather, a name that won't repel
But brings confidence and bounce

My mother should have examined then
And don't call me Cinderella or Sarefa
Just give me a nice likkle pretty name
Like Jennifer Patrecia

Naming a child can make or break
Someone from the very start
Mek Mona Lisa siddung one side
It's just a lonely work of art.

Likkle Bow-Leg Steve

Memba likkle bow-leg Steve
Miss Babba wah ded, last son?
Me see 'im just the other day
Saying to a nice lady "Yes Hon"

I thought I recognized de voice
But now it get so deep
Miss Babba wouldda proud a 'im
If she wake up out of her sleep

He is the perfect son I know
The one we never had
From birth that's just how he was
Miss Babba heart must glad

Now when you look pon Steve bow leg
'Im stand up straight and good
A nice wide smile, strong nails and teeth
Miss Babba fed him good food

Dat young lady weh have him fi husband
Betta tek good care fi keep
A man so respectable an' nice
From wolf wa look lakka sheep

'Cause if dem evva ketch poor Steve
Wid his bright future ahead
Dem might nuh treat 'im wonderful
Miss Babba wouldda raise fram di dead

Me personally wouldda vex
Mi heart wouldda skip a beat
Fi see likkle bow leg Steve tun man
Wid leggo beas pon street

'Im nuh know rough life at all missis
Miss Babba tek every care
Some tings wah she do fid dat de son
Fi Steve dat was good an' fair

She was a nice lady wid a nice son
Coming from a umble staat
Mi feel suh proud an is not my chile
It wouldda warm Miss Babba heart.

Jamaican Games Once Played

"I am a pretty little Dutch girl," we always used to play
Right up deh suh a Paradise Row, best part of Montego Bay
Di prettiest girls play dally house, wid English cup and saucer
Mek Jonkro bead bracelet, recite poem an' even read some Chaucer

An a ongle wan likkle girl, did have a real-real dolly house
She live inna di bigges' yaad, an quiet lakka mouse
She wave fram di verandah, wen wi pass on di way home
Suh we a lang fi go inna har yaad, a suh she long fi roam

Wi mek paper kite an boat and den play slip-not-there
But wen dem play a-bungle-up, mi nuh really like go near
Wi sew dally clothes wid scrappsies, plait coc"nat leaf mek belt
A game a roundas inna hat sun, mek you feel like yuh aggo melt

When we have hoola-hoop contest, mi mek sure seh mi win
Mi neck, mi han, mi wais, mi foot, den back up to mi chin
It tek some skill and nuff practice fi dis art form get refined
Wen yuh a compete 'gainst di bes, yuh train both body an mind

Di boys play football and cyad, and some go shoot bird a bush
Dem run a boat an plat wis, while di girls dem siddung stush
Dem mek telephone outta candense can, an wan piece a sash card
Fi tek ol pan and catton reel mek truck, is a real gift from God

A nuff tings Jamaican pickney invent, wid accuracy and insight
We could'n just get up go buy toys, for things were rather tight
So we play jacks an marble, wi play yoyo an mek wi owna gig
Wi play ring aroun di roses, wi hopscotch, skip, dance and jig

Spin the bottle, Chinese checkers, dart, ludo and dandy shandy
Cricket, race and run go swim; thank God we were so handy
You see all dat same breadfruit sword, wi tek it an mek doll
Wi plait up one anadda hair, entertainment for one and all

You memba concentration, well we used to play dat too
Mi cyaan possibly rememba all di things dat wi used to do
Sometime wen wi get well tiad we staat play hide an seek
Conserve sum strength fi later, when wi staat kin pup-a-lik

Nuh Mek Bad Tawt Linga

Teller: You are next, may I help yuh ma'am? (fi ar yeye dem big lakka pattuh)
Customer: Yes, yes please. (Mi wait lang 'nuff) A want to mek a ladgement to mi savins. Ere is the book an ere is di money. (ope she urry up, caa mi cyaan linga yasso tidday)
Teller: Ok, let me check the money and then do the transaction. (lawks, dis smell like it wen inna ol boot an it nat even inna no awda, pschoew)
Customer: Everything aright pretty girl? (tink shi cute, a bet shi ansa) Tekking yuh a lang time fi count di likkle money. (ol dunce, all manner of people wuk inna bank dese days.)
Teller: Yes, yes everything's just fine. Doing my best to get you out. (Nuh even badda try urry mi caa di money sticky-sticky an frowzy lakka stale doockoonu. Jus mek mi deal wid dis so yu cyan urry up leff) It was pleasure to serve you. Here you go Miss.
Customer: Mrs. That is Mrs. Evangelina Serafina Pestiguru married over 20 years wid two nice bright sons at University. Yuh wouldda nuff, 'bout 'Miss.'
Teller: My apologies Mrs. PEST-iguru. (Di son dem mus tek afta di faada if she she dem nice) Do have a pleasant day. (ope yuh slide outta street an drap)
Customer: No problem. (ol pappy show) A hope a get yuh di next time a come (so a cyan trace yuh an report yuh to yuh baass fi call mi MISS)
Teller: Take care Mrs. Pestiguru (look like a jeng jeng)
Customer: ok likkle miss (she mawga lakka dawg an har clothes set like it heng pon nail. She a go have a warm time fi fine usban. A hope ar pike eel bruk.)

Teller: [afterthought]
Dat mus be mi bwayfren madda , dem las name is di same
Is not a common name at all, oh lawks a feelin very shame
Is wat I gwine go tell har when mi bwayfren cyarry mi 'ome
Fi go meet im daalin madda wah him cherish to har bone?

Customer: [afterthought]
Mi mine a tell mi supp'm strange an mi nuh tink it wrang
Caas it nuh stap repeat suh till it almost tun inna sang
Mi son seh im did like a slim girl weh work inna wan bank
An fram all a who mi see in deh she is really di top rank

Teller & Customer [afterthought]
Well she will be a paat of mi life, and so from dis day fort,
I not gwine mek no bad tings linga, only pleasant thoughts
Cause yuh doan really know who might cum into yuh life
An all yuh want is peace and love. Nuh badda wid di strife.

Willy Penny

Sell mi faad'n wut a sugar an ay-p'ny wut a rice
An gil wut a caanmeal, lawks mi haffi watch di price
Caas a living gawn up suh high, ah wa wi aggo duh
Saalfish haffi go siddung wait, an di cookin ayl it to

Cut mi penny wut a haadough an before yuh add it up
Ah waan quatty wut a plaintain an red peas wid di tup
Serve mi chuppance a di saal poke and memba di butta
Spen di groat and mi still nuh get onion, salt an di peppa

Tanner a same as sixpance, fi keep mi packet waam
Yuh also ave di shillin, dat yuh use fi keep aaff haam
Florin, same as two Shillin, an nex is half a crown
Dat two an six and afta dat five shillin mek a crown

A half poun fi cough syrup now, a ten big shillin dat
Yuh cyaan even afford fi sick, an cyaan buy pretty 'at
A wan poun fi buy medicine dung a di cheapis dispensa
An wan guinea fi a good lawyer or fi retain a barrista

Well I doan haffi worry now, mi son deh a university
An every week afta 'im done, gwine earn a half guinea
'Im gwine save money inna bank, caas 'im is very willin
Fi help me get mi own guinea, wholla twenty one shilling

But put all fun an joke aside, yuh memba wen yuh likkle
Di kine wa wi nuh talk 'bout yet, used to provide nuff bikkle
As simple as dis penny soun an tink it nuh wut a win
Shine an pallish it wan day an go dung a Missa Chin

Yuh buy bulla an bun an cheese an some kola champagne
An treat yuh fren to titti bread wid butta; oh what a game
Di bes time is wen it get busy, usually pon a Friday nite
Im wan serve big people an get di pickney dem outta site

Wen yuh buy all a wah yuh want an get all change fram dis
Yuh laugh cause Missa Chin get Willy an tink a two an six
Den nex week Friday di same ting yuh game jus nevva en
Yuh smile an place yuh aada fi both yusself an fi yuh fren

Willy penny have adda uses, as I got much olda I would fine
Dat is a simple Willy penny, but is worth a whole gold mine
An if baby have big nable an yuh want di swellin fi go weh
Tie aan a copper Willy an yuh wanda weh di swellin deh

Tank God we learn fi count money, pounds, shillings an pence
But people seh Jamaica gwine soon use ongle dallaz and cents
Den wah gwine happen to po' Willy, piece of copper so distinct
Special penny wid summuch uses, gwine soon become extinct.

Faad'n = Farthing (fourth of a thing) = ¼ penny or ¼ d
Ay-p'ny = Half penny (Hay-p'ny) = ½ d
Gil = Farthing and half penny = ¾ d
Penny = 1d (twelve of these make a shilling)
Quatty = Penny+half penny (penny hay-p'ny) = 1+1/4d
Tup = tuppance = two pence = 2d
Chuppance = tropense = Three pence = 3d
Groat = = four pence = 4d
Tanner = Sixpance = sixpence = half shilling = 6d
Florin = shilling = s1
Two-bob bit = two shillings = s2
Half crown = two and six = two shillings and six pence = 2s/6d
Crown = five shillings = 5s
Half pound = ten shillings = 10s
Half guinea = ten and six = ten shillings and six pence = 10s/6d
Pound = quid = twenty shillings = 20s = £1.
Guinea = twenty one shillings = 21s = £1.1s
Shilling = s1 = 12d
Florin = two shillings= s2

Old time Willy penny

Jennifer P. Lumley

Flowaz Afta Howaz

Wah yuh ask mi seh di adda day, 'bout di girl yuh si mi wid
Yuh waan fi know her name an ting, an fine out if she married?
Yuh waan fi know if yuh cyan send a bunch a pretty flowaz
Or if yuh can meet up wid her one day fi have dinna afta howaz?

Wah yuh seh 'bout dis perfect place, wah yuh have pon yuh mine
Fi tek dis freshly-picked looking flower, dis damsel so refine?
Yuh ask mi how her lipliner is always so perfectly in place
Well chosen clothes, beautifully worn, down to her very shoe lace

I mus admit yuh really sharp, mi fren, yuh admire true beauty
One gentle smile and shake of hands, gave you a sense of duty.
All dem compliment yuh paid, try yuh bes, nat even badda
The girl you met you'll see har again, that lady is mi madda.

Patois Reference

Patois is a dynamic language attuned primarily to accents and dialects. It, therefore, has several words with the same meaning as well as single word having several meanings. The 14 parishes in Jamaica and even the towns and districts of those parishes, possess their indigenous patois form. In Kingston alone, there is 'uptown' and 'downtown' patois, carefully spoken to be deliberately different. Certainly, what has been captured in these few pieces does not represent the basilect, mesolect or acrolect studies of patois; only the gist of the plethora of words and expressions, used by Jamaicans...till tomorrow when something else is added.

A = I
Aan = on
Adda = other
Afta = after
Afta howaz = late evening
Aggo = going to
An = and
Attrack = attract
Awda = order
Ays = ears
Badda = bother
Bax = box/slap in the face
Bax front = O my gosh
Behavia = behavior
Betta = better
Bigges = biggest
Brawta = a little extra
Brawta = unexpectedly free
Brawta = no cost

Brawta = gratis
Breadfruit sword = a shoot from the tree
Bway = boy
Calla = colour
Candense can = tin can
Caw = because
College = college
Catton reel = thread spool
'Cause = because
Chat = talk
Claat = cloth
Choo = through
Coc'nat = coconut
Coob up = cooped up
Cudda – could have
Cyad = card game
Cyan = can
Cyaan = cannot

Dat = that

Deggay-deggay = only/single

Dem = them

Di = the

Di adda day = the other day

Dis = this

Dissa = this here

Dundus = albino/fair skin

Dung a grung = down on the ground

Een = in

Evva = ever

Ess = esses

Fa = because/for

Fartune = fortune

Fi = for

Fi kiss = to kiss

Fine = find

Finga = finger

Flava = flavor

Flowaz = flowers

Fooley-fooley = very foolish/ stupid

'fraid = afraid

Frak = frock/dress

Fram = from

Fren = friend

'Gainst = against

Gawn = gone

Gi = give

Good-good = very good

Gwine = going to

Haffi = have to

Han = hand

Har = her

Hat = hot

Im = him

Inna = into/in

Jai = joy

Jankro bead = decorative black & red bead

Jus = just

Kerchief = handkerchief

Ketch - catch

Kinda = kind of

Kin pup–a-lik = cartwheel/ somersault

Lakka = like a

Lattery = lottery

Lawd = Lord

Leggo beas = loose person (esp. woman)

Liad = liar

Lick = hit

Likkle = little

Madda = mother

Mawnin = morning

Memba = remember

Mek = make

'Merica = America

Mi = my

Mighta = might

Missis = denotes female (single or married)

Mout = mouth

Mus = must

Nat = not

Neighba = neighbor

Nevva = never

Nice-nice = especially nice

Nize = noise

Nuff = plentiful/many

Nuh = don't

Nuh stap ya so = unbelieveable

Nuttin' = nothing

One anadda = each another

Ongle = only

Ooman = woman

Oonu = you all/everyone

Outta = out of

Owna = own

Packet = pocket

Parridge = porridge

Pickcha = picture

Pickney = child

Pon = on

Pschoew = expresses disgust/
anger/

Rememba = remember

Rounna = around the

Roundas = rounders (like
baseball)

Run boat = crude outdoor
cooking

Seh = say

Si = see

Siddung = sit down

Shudda = should have

Smaddy = somebody

Soun = sound

Staat = start

Strang = strong

Stush = Proper

Suh = So

Summuch = so much/many

Tappy = stop the (noise)

Tek = take

Tetnus shat = tetanus shot

Tink = think

Tun = turn

Tyad = tired

Waan = want

Wa = who/what

Wah = who/what

Wat = what

Wata = water

Weh I deh = where is it

Wen = when

Wid = with

Wudda = would have

Wut = worth

Yaad = yard

Yuh = you/your